A Bite-Sized Public Affairs Book

China and the West

Unravelling 100 Years of Misunderstanding

揭开中西百年误解

Yue He Parkinson （何越）

Cover by

Dean Stockton

Published by Bite-Sized Books Ltd 2021
©Yue He Parkinson 2021

Bite-Sized Books Ltd 8th Floor, 20 St. Andrews Street, London EC4A 3AY, UK

Registered in the UK. Company Registration No: 9395379

ISBN: 9798767807871

The moral right of Yue He Parkinson to be identified as the author of this work has been asserted by her in accordance with the Copyright, Designs and Patents Act 1988

Although the publisher, editors and authors have used reasonable care in preparing this book, the information it contains is distributed as is and without warranties of any kind. This book is not intended as legal, financial, social or technical advice and not all recommendations may be suitable for your situation. Professional advisors should be consulted as needed. Neither the publisher nor the author shall be liable for any costs, expenses or damages resulting from use of or reliance on the information contained in this book.

*For my husband Marcus and our
daughters Meili & Angelina*

China and the West, by Yue Parkinson is a succinct, erudite and concise piece of writing about contemporary China and its politics today. Her clear explanation about how it functions, with fascinating historical references, makes it one of the most enlightening books I have read in ages about the subject. Witty at the same time, this book is a reading delight. Without a doubt, it should be required reading for diplomats as well as anyone who wants to do business in China.

Ken Hom, OBE

Contents

Foreword	1
Vince Cable	
Introduction	4
Chapter 1	12
Why is it a revenge?	
Chapter 2	37
How did America's reliance on China happen?	
Chapter 3	46
Why is China challenging the US now?	
Chapter 4	69
How did the misunderstanding between China and the West happen?	
Chapter 5	85
Conclusion	
Postscript	97

Foreword

Vince Cable

Any book which starts with a positive reference to 'racial pride' is either written to provoke outrage in a politically correct, liberal, readership or is written in a fundamentally different idiom which doesn't recognise Western norms and sensitivities. Yue Parkinson's book on China, written from the standpoint of a Chinese journalist, who has lived in the West and has a British husband, attempts – bravely and, I think, successfully – to get under the skin of Chinese and Western attitudes and prejudices and explain them.

The book is quite unlike, in both style and content, the analytical tomes on China written by Western academics and commentators (including me). It is raw and authentic. It describes the mental map which she grew up with and is followed by her Chinese friends and how it has remained and also changed, for her, as a result of two decades' deep immersion in British society. She is clearly more comfortable in the Chinese language than English (she wrote for the FT for Chinese readers), but that doesn't detract from the freshness and honesty of the book.

She explains some key concepts which are difficult for Westerners to get their heads around. 'Dayitong', roughly translated as a high level of autocracy, underpins the emperor-like status of Xi Jinping. 'Yangren', roughly translated as 'white foreigners', conveys both hatred and admiration and is associated with a Chinese quest for revenge after the century of semi-colonialism. The Chinese embrace 'human rights' but mean something quite different: economic improvements and security (as in the protection provided by ferocious Covid 'lock-downs'.

She has some important new ideas: Chinese women 'voting with their wombs' against the competitive pressures which require them to strive and leave little scope for more children. Indeed, that is her explanation for Xi's sudden change of policy direction to emphasise 'common prosperity'. Another is her depiction of Chinese national pride as like the assertion of Black Lives Matter at an international level.

The book does not fuel optimism. There is a fundamental divide between societies based on individualism and China's fierce sense of national pride and duty. China's approach to 'territorial integrity' - i.e. Hong Kong and Taiwan - is a 'holy task even at the expense of war'. Hostility is met by hostility. There are many Chinese, as well as Americans, who see ahead a life and death struggle for hegemon power.

This is an important book.

Vince Cable

Sir Vince Cable, British politician and former Leader of the Liberal Democrats and Secretary of State for Business, Innovation and Skills

Introduction

Racial and national pride is the most powerful patriotic emotion that unites the Chinese against the USA. Having felt bullied by the Yangren (white people) for over 100 years, overtaking the US is a matter of revenge for the Chinese, who have been learning about the historical humiliation of China via 'patriotic' education (in which the Opium War of 1839 has been the leading tune). Rather than a successful national model, grown in and benefitting from the international system led by the US, China has taken itself as a victim under the Western and American control. Thus, the national interest of defeating the US has turned into the whole country's individual interest and duty as well.

The ingenuity of this Chinese revenge is that American businessmen have stood by China's side, a justifiable decision defined by the economic globalization led by the US for decades. The competition between China and the US is a new style competition of world power, not only by science and technology, but also by trade and businesses. For the supporters of economic globalization (e.g., China) the competition is a setback; for the supporters of globalization, politically, economically, and culturally, (e.g., the US) it's a must fight after waking up to the cost of economic globalization.

China has developed a powerful and efficient strategy based on national capitalism growing links and twists within the world economy. As the strongest supporter for the economic globalization, China so far has been dominating the global supply chain. In other words, parts of China's resources have relied on Western customers purchasing Made-in-China products based on the spirit of consumerism, businessmen investing in China as the most stable and profitable place, as well as Chinese factories providing the cheapest labour, weak labour laws, and no unions.

Is China a developing country? By the definition of the WTO, yes. Yet how can a developing country compete with the US? Surely China is a *developed* country? Even so, can a *statist* country compete with a democratic country based on foreign policy? This seems against the evolving trend of the world. Thousands of years of world politics has witnessed three transformations, from religion-centred, to nation-centred (statism), and to individual-centred (human rights). Europe was the first continent which finished the three transformations, and finally turned into a peaceful land. China turned into a statist nation during the Qin Dynasty 2,000 ago, and still is.

The truth is that the trend the US had led for almost 70 years, pushing political, economic and cultural globalization forward, stopped in 2016. We are witnessing history: either economic globalization carries on if China wins, or, political globalization carries on if the US wins. The harmony between political and economic development has disappeared.

Covid-19 has seen deep reliance on China when the West failed even to self-manufacture facemasks, yet not every American realized that the US has recently become the victim of free trade and globalization.

For the last four decades, welcomed by the US, Chinese economic progress had been taken as a positive step for the promotion of full-scale globalization, a potential stage leading to Chinese political reform. The Trump government was the first US government that realized the former judgement was wrong, because China had made up its mind up long way before – never follow the West in political approach. Trump intended to break the US's reliance on China, yet it proved unbelievably hard.

Now Biden's government is focusing on protecting its fundamental supply chain, a small percentage among all US economic links with China. The US has been trying to unite with its allies in the name of human rights, especially Xingjian genocide, and national security, perhaps even the origin of the Covid-19. So far Australia, Canada, the UK, and the EU have all reacted to China with a strong political stance, yet it hasn't really reflected on the economic movement. China is still growing fast.

In general, economic movement in the US is free from politics, which has led to an ironic fact: US citizens are helping China to defeat the US. A certain spirit of national interest or personal duty is missing in the US. How did these bizarre things happen?

1. A dilemma between the welfare system and profit-driven business model, or a dilemma between democracy and capitalism. Exploiting the cheap labour in China was a way out to escape this dilemma, yet it has proved to be a bad move which may finally damage the hegemonic status of the US on the world stage.

2. China has been mobilising the whole country to pursue profit, which has turned the majority into businessmen who have made millions or even billions through links with the US. This allows them to lobby American domestic politics, control domestic jobs, people's life quality, and more.

3. The foundation of economic globalization is political globalization, yet its development is far behind the progress of the economic globalization.

It's a competition between American individual interests and individual duties which China has embraced for over 2,000 years. Human rights are the principle in the US, and these duties are mainly carried out by the nation. If China wins, it will imply that using the principle of human rights to rule the world encounters a serious historical obstacle.

It's also a competition about who is able to unite its people the most, no matter how cruel the approach is. For the US, so far the idea is to unite its allies through human rights, law, and democracy. Yet compared to China, in the US it is much harder to unite Americans for the following reasons:

1. The deep dependence on Chinese economy.

2. The freedom of speech and the diversity of opinions on social media, while China controls the media and social media, and blocks Western websites such as Google, Facebook, Twitter, the BBC, etc.

3. The high standard of human rights makes the cost of domestic maintenance much higher than in China, where there are still

"600 million people whose monthly income was barely 1,000 yuan ($154)" according to Chinese Premier Li Keqiang in 2020.[1] Despite this, very few complain.

4. American people care about animal rights, climate change, refugees, individual interests, party interest, community interest, etc, but not so much about their national interest or duty.

China is a world the US hasn't spent enough time and effort researching fully. The Chinese government has been encouraging its people to carry on doing businesses with the West, and going abroad to study and invest, all of which has turned into resources of Chinese power; yet since the West has bullied China before and are against China's growing stronger, on the 26th April 2021, Xi reminded the whole nation of the fighting spirit of the Red Army: "Red Army soldiers stayed fearless in the face of death, with strong ideals and convictions…We should have such beliefs in achieving the second centenary goal and realizing national rejuvenation". Xi went on to ask that "In the face of even greater difficulty, think about the Long March and the Xiangjiang battle",[2] invoking the need to sacrifice self-interest for the sake of serving Chinese national interest - a mindset similar to the British spirit during the two World Wars.

It's a competition between the 1.3 billion obedient Chinese citizens who follow orders unconditionally in political, economic, and cultural ways, and the US people who claim strong individual rights and have less confidence in the government, who actually stand by the Chinese side unconsciously. It's a revenge for China. The loser will be either economic globalization, or democracy.

Chapter 1
Why is it a revenge?

On the 2nd of May 2021, the U.S. Secretary of State Antony Blinken said of China in the CBS show *60 Minutes*: "It is the one country in the world that has the military, economic, diplomatic capacity to undermine or challenge the rules-based order that we - we care so much about and arc determined to defend over time." He also said: "China believes that it […] can be and should be and will be the dominant country in the world."[1]

US-Sino relations have turned into a clear and direct competition after the Alaska meeting in March 2021. So far, China has teamed up with Russia, Iran, and the UAE in trying to organize a new ally to confront the Western human rights standard.

The seed of revenge was planted in 1839, when the British Empire launched the first Opium War on China, which led to the 99 years rent of Hong Kong to the empire. From early in the 20th Century, the disgrace, humiliation, and shame from this War has become a political symbol in Chinese patriotic education. Reviving China has been the national slogan. Chairman Mao called to overtake the UK and US in the 1950s. The Xinhua News Agency published due to the correct Chinese political approach, that "We have been overtaking the UK and US before Xi visited the UK where he would be received by the queen with an overwhelmingly honour" in 2015[2].

Since Americans did not colonise China, what is the reason for the revenge against them? 'Yangren', a word said by Yang Jiechi (a member of the Political Bureau of the CPC Central Committee and director of the Office of the Foreign Affairs Commission of the CPC Central Committee) during the Alaska meeting was absolutely missed by the Western media. The full sentence he said was: "We have suffered enough from the pain caused by Yangren." Yangren was an old Chinese noun during the colonization era, specifically meaning white people (occasionally including Japanese) who semi-colonized China. It was a positive word when China looked up to the white people yet has turned into a negative image recalling humiliation. "We have suffered enough from the pain caused by Yangren" was received overwhelmingly well in domestic China, who found it a victorious moment where the Chinese were finally able to stand up to the West. It's revenge not just on the US, but the whole Western world, led by the US.

On the 7th of May 2021, the Xinhua News Agency published a photo of the collective leaders of G7 countries, yet the clothing of the leaders was changed to the old style of the colonial era. The caption read "this group of people last gathered together in 1900. 120 years have passed, are they still dreaming of bullying us?"[3] Again, this was another way for the media to unite the Chinese people, alerting them to the similarity between the West's actions of the past, and the present.

Neglected by the West, the post-colonial feeling of hatred has never been, and will never be, forgotten by not only China but all former semi-colonized and colonized countries. This will remain until they are equal to the West, or even superior. This strong sentiment can be seen as one kind of human rights, about which the US has no clue. I would like to call it a right of racial national pride, which has been a matter of national importance for China – on par with the Black Lives Matter movement in the USA.

Misunderstanding China

It's the Chinese 2,000 years old political system of Dayitong(大一统), the highest level of autocracy, that is competing with the US.

China was considered Communist simply because China followed the Soviet Union in the 20th century, a practice which only lasted for a few decades.

Recently Joe Biden used the terms democracy versus autocracy to describe the competition between the US and China, yet autocracy is the main reason for China's rise. In fact, the proper name for the Chinese political system is Da(big) Yi(one) Tong (unification). There is no proper English translation for it, but it means the unification through politics, the economy, values, and movements, and can be understood as the highest level of autocracy. For the last 2,000 years, Chinese dynasties have risen and died, yet they all adopted the policy of Dayitong, which proved to be efficient and powerful at the beginning of building a new country, yet all ended with demise. The Chinese Communist Party has also adopted the Dayitong. The Cultural Revolution, the success of economic performances and the success of implementing the Zero tolerance policy to Covid-19 are all the results of Dayitong From my own 16 years of experience living in the UK, I figured out that Chinese society in the 21st Century is very much similar to the British society in the 18th Century, when money and social status were the main social pursuit. However, I'm sure that there is no similar way for the US to understand China because they have not much in common except trade. The Chinese love to say that life is like chess. Chinese autocracy supports one player who sets up the whole strategy to play all way through until he dies, yet America has to change the player every 4/8 years.

The most powerful person is China is often called 'president' of China, but this is in fact a misnomer. Xi Jinping, the most powerful person in China is in fact called 'The Paramount Leader'. In general, he owns three leadership roles — head of the Communist Party, military and state - at the same time, although the former Paramount Leader Deng Xiaoping from the end of 1970s to 1990s didn't carry any of these roles. The most important role among these is the head of the Communist Party, a position elected by the Politburo Standing Committee (PSC)rather than the members of the Communist Party. The position of the 'President' is a name convenient for the Paramount Leader's visits to other nations.

The so-called 'president' of the nation and the chairman of the military are selected every five years by the National People's Congress (NPC), who are selected by indirect election, which what leads Biden to use the term 'autocracy'.

Why didn't Chinese politics change to democracy?

It's naive for Clinton, Bush and Obama to believe that a strong Chinese economy will lead to democracy. The US political system is the polar opposite of the Chinese statist system. In the US, people are far more empowered than the Chinese population. All Chinese power comes from the Paramount leader, who controls all of the national resources including media, forces, and courts. The advantage for the US system is that the majority of individual interests can be satisfied, while the national interest is in the second place. Conversely, China prioritises national benefits while leaving individual interests to the wayside.

Seen as natural rights, democracy and human rights have been taken for granted by Western people. British friends used to ask me: "Why doesn't China have democracy?", in the same tone as "why don't they eat cake?". The West don't know how lucky they are, because their ancestors embraced the ideas from the Enlighten movement, and turned statism to individualism, a journey admired by some Chinese citizens for over 100 years. It isn't a natural right at all.

The case of the first generation of Chinese immigrants living in the UK can prove how hard it is for the Chinese to comprehend democracy and human rights. Duc to the national patriotic education in China, all Chinese immigrants will feel guilty immediately if they say they love the country where they are living. They unconsciously self-censor their comments about China, and protect the image of China unconditionally. Their common behaviour is: studying and working extremely hard because they believe Social Darwinism dominates Western society; having no ideas of social benefits; regarding people applying for state benefits as shameful; embracing and supporting the government (whichever party is in power); regarding the protection of free media as a bad thing; highly emphasising the importance of private education; hoping their children can be at the top of British society at the cost of others; intolerance of other races, etc. They rarely have ideas about how to improve and reform society, as the logic learned from China teaches them that this is an issue reserved only for the Government.

For 100 years, there has been a popular turn of phrase in China calling for the country to follow science and democracy, in the same footsteps as the West. So far, it looks like science has finally arrived in China, but not democracy. I have researched the whole process of British democracy from birth to the present: it is an impossible journey for China to imitate, as is the birth of American democracy. Democracy entails empowering the population of a country, so either the Chinese leader must be willing to relinquish autocratic power, or the people must ask for power by violent or peaceful ways (none of which have happened in China since 1989).

Chinese politics is called Chinese character Socialism, a mixture of Marxism illustrated by Russian communism, National Capitalism, and the traditional Chinese imperial style **Dayitong**. Based on Statism, it's the most practical and flexible theory without any hindrance by religion, ideologies, or human rights, aiming only for money and national power.

Marxism lay the foundation for the Chinese Community Party to seize power by violence in 1949, and has thus been called the basis of Chinese character Socialism. Ironically, Chinese national capitalism is similar to the cruel British capitalism of the

19th century which was severely criticized by Marxism. Also, because the Marxism in China was pioneered by Russia first, only few Chinese people really know what true Marxism is. It has been a useful name and theory to unite Chinese anyway.

Like contemporary North Korea, China was very poor before 1978 China finally changed its enclosure policy to get involved in the world economy. My English husband and I were both born in the 1970s He compared my childhood to an African child, which shocked me, because we were told we were the luckiest and happiest people in the world. I did not depict my childhood in that bad way, because everyone was equal, and society looked fair. No-one was rich, but no-one was poor.

Due to the then two leaders, Hu Yaobang and Zhao Ziyang, the 1980s were the rare open and free times for the Chinese after the Chinese Communist Party had been in power since 1949. New ideas like democracy, freedom of speech, etc were introduced into China, and Chinese students embraced them heavily. Anyone who was able to study or even emigrate to the US would be hugely envied. We all looked up to the US like a heaven where gold could be picked up as you were walking. We had never heard of racism in the US then. When I saw the news of Syrian refugees being smuggled across the British Channel to the UK, it always reminded me of Cantonese smuggled from the Shenzhen River to Hong Kong in the 1970s and 1980s. It's a worthy risk when there is no life in your hometown.

The Tiananmen Square protest in 1989 stopped the pursuit of Western ideas, which were taken as a threat to the government. At that time, China regarded the West as the epitome of capitalism, which was a bad word in China between 1949 to about 1978 (when the farmers and the workers were the hero and superior group of people, and businessmen were the sinners). In 1992, Deng Xiaoping made a decision to change China from a planned market to a free market. He said: "The Planned economy doesn't mean socialism, capitalism has a planned economy as well; the market economy doesn't mean capitalism, socialism has a market economy as well".[4] Very soon, the dominating social value became money; the former sinner entrepreneurs turned into social stars, and the former heroes such as farmers and workers became the losers.

Adam Smith's idea of the invisible hand became very popular in China in the 1990s. All of sudden the planned market turned from positive to negative after a long and hot debate about which is the best, planned market or free market. I only found out the UK adopted democratic socialism between 1945 to 1979 in 2016 after I had settled down in the UK for 12 years. British democratic socialism was unheard of in China, as China had closed itself from the world from 1949 to 1978, and has not really caught up with the modern world, meaning the UK are still taken as having the most distinct class system of any country even today. Because the majority of research funds in Chinese universities are focused on American politics and society, I became the first Chinese reporter to tell Chinese readers of the FT Chinese that the aristocracy system had long gone in the UK. A reporter from Chinese state media interviewed me specifically on this issue and could not believe that the aristocracy now need to work to live. When I told my Chinese friends that then Labour leader Corbyn is a socialist, she was shocked, and asked: "the planned market is bad, why does the UK still want it?" For Chinese people, "the West" means the US, the UK, other European nations, etc. Even the US and the UK are viewed as the same country for all intents and purposes: both are capitalist, which means ruthless. Even by now, many Chinese citizens believe that socialism is a euphemism for China. At the same time, the welfare system in the West is taken as a policy making people lazy thus weaken the national power.

China was an oligarchy from 1993 to 2013 when Jiang Zeming and Hu Jingtao were in power. It's believed this was a tiny move towards democracy, yet this ultimately failed.

Why doesn't China embrace human rights?

While the Enlightenment movement turned European counties from nation-centred to individual-centred, China has been a land where the Enlightenment revolution has never shed its light, a land where the leader has been taken as the most prestigious and moral person for over two thousand years.

Are human rights all equal? American Secretary of State Antony Blinken said yes, claiming "Human rights are also co-equal. There is no hierarchy that makes some rights more important than others".[5] Yet the Chinese government says otherwise. China has embraced a hierarchical system of human rights, in which two kinds of rights have been the highlights: economic rights and security rights in the Covid-19 battle. Many Chinese citizens believed that China has enjoyed the highest standard of human rights during the Pandemic. A popular question I was often asked was: "if the UK really cares about human rights, why was their death toll over 120,000?" There was an argument about whether China should adapt to live with the Covid-19 in the middle of 2021, yet soon the consent of a Zero Tolerance policy was achieved by the power of Dayitong, However, so far, some Chinese have become fed up with the tough and strict Zero Tolerance policy since China had closed its border already for over 18 months. Meanwhile, large numbers of overseas Chinese, including me, could not afford to go back to China due to the complicating tests, and the expensive and long hotel quarantine obligations. I haven't seen my mother in Guangzhou, who suffered from stroke, over two years. From the Western perspective, it's not humane, yet the majority Chinese believe it's justifiable as the individual interest has to defer to the collective interest/national interest.

Why don't the Chinese embrace the full scale of human rights first, and then move on to revenge against the US? The Chinese government has strongly believed that the freedom of speech, and to protest, and other rights will decrease economic efficiency, which is much more important than fairness and equality. Other rights have to wait.

Can China fully embrace human rights at the same time as revenge? No. Because the West has proved that the more equal and fairer a society is, the less sense of danger the people will feel, the more relaxed people will be, and the less hard people will work. The precondition for defeating the US is that Chinese people have to carry on working as hard as before, or even harder, without the protection of a welfare system, under an extremely strong competitive environment in which the gap between rich and poor is wide. This, however, cruelly, has been the strongest push for the production ability and invention.

To the West's surprise, since the Chinese people have been believing that the resources of power come from authority, the more rights they are offered by the government, the happier Chinese will be. Nowadays, because China is getting richer and richer, people are more confident and happier than before. In the meantime, they suffer from severe domestic competition, which is reflected by the two most popular new words in 2021, Neijuan（内卷）and Tangping（躺平）.

Neijuan is the translation from involution, under Chinese circumstance. It means that no matter how much effort people put into work, the result will be the about the same since the competition has been so fierce, there is no hope for a better life in the future when people are willing to work harder at any cost.

Tangping means to lie down and refuse to work as hard as before, which is the consequence from Neijuan. These two popular words can vividly explain the Chinese people's true emotion, which was caused by the four decades of radical economic reform-at-any-cost. On the one hand, people are happy because they are richer; on the other hand, people are exhausted as life has become much harder mentally and physically. The co-existence of these two extreme feelings of happiness and anxiety, are very much like the Chinese feelings about the Yangren; admiration mixed with hatred.

The most shocking fact was that after the central government finally allowed people to have the third child, the response was a collective NO. They said it's too expensive and hard to raise a second child, let alone the third one, because children's lives became studying machines day and night for the sake of winning in the most competitive society; to getting into the best schools, universities, and careers. Parents, so called tiger parents, have no time for themselves as they have to take the kids to different educational classes after school every day. The majority of British Mainland Chinese parents continued this way for their kids. They complained about their busy and hard life because they could never be relaxed until their kids became the elites in the UK.

They also look down on British parents' attitude to education – why don't they try their best to send the kids to the private schools which will pave the way to the top of society? Don't they care about their kids' future? Judged by the Chinese standard, British parents are too laid back, too irresponsible, and too selfish. As someone who's been living in the middle between the UK and China, I can understand both attitudes.

For a long, long time, Chinese people have had no way to have any say about the national policy which was in the hands of the central government. Yet this time, a magic thing happened after people refused to be pregnant – they voted by their wombs to say No to the government. I will name it 'Wombs Vote' in the rest of this book. In the summer of 2021, Xi launched a series of campaigns directed against the richest private companies, such as Didi, Alibaba, Tencent, etc, and also towards private teaching auxiliary institutions, video games addiction, celebrity worship, all of which was explained as the second Cultural Revolution by some Western media. Yet I understand these campaigns are the huge causes of the serious social problems results arising from the Wombs Vote, because the government suddenly realized that it was impossible to maintain domestic stability and sustainability of China itself without sorting out the worry and concern in people's minds that made them prefer to give up having a child – a unheard of situation and hard to comprehend for the West. The radical social reform on a giant scale, for the time being, is very Chinese in style, and can only be launched by Dayitong government, one capable of locking down Wuhan overnight.

Apart from Wombs Vote, another reason for the current Chinese hurricane style reforms is to upgrade Chinese industry and force the investment from the industries which were banned or rectified recently – educational, real estate, infrastructure, internet, etc - to the new and strategy industries, say semi-conductor, green energy, etc, which will enable China to compete with the US in the long term.

Also, the rectification of the celebrity worship and the Hupan University founded by Jack Ma were the signs of preventing from the potential strong challenge groups to the government.

Yet how on earth didn't the Chinese government figure out the huge social problem of *Wombs Vote* when their people are tired, disappointed and trying to give up? It doesn't make sense in the Western society as any equivalent complaints and dissatisfaction would be show up quickly on social media and human rights-oriented media. The answer is simple – Chinese media run by the state are only allowed to report good and positive news, so as to show that China has been making rapid progress. It's true, yet the negative consequence has been that the country has no way to observe the social trouble until it breaks out like a violent volcano – a view held by the Wombs Vote. I used to think how tolerant Chinese were at facing up to the hardship, from my parents' generation to my own generation, as I can see that no Westerners, who enjoy more rights than obligations, can accept these kinds of strong commitments to the nation, family, and the kids, would complain and resist. I know I could not now survive in China no matter how rich China could become as I have lost the ability to be tolerant – the UK has taught me how to fight for my own interests and rights, which is a worrying thing because it has started to tip over a line leading to damaging the national interest.

Therefore, suddenly, 'common prosperity（共同富裕）' became the most important political key words from the summer of 2021. Those last four decades of the pursuit of money have slowed down, sharing money has started to become a social idea. At the moment asking a rich company to donate money to the society in a charitable way, as opposed to a welfare system, was the way out. Because of the Christian influence, the tradition for the rich to donate money to the charity has been long and deep in the West. Chinese society has been influenced by Confucianism, in which politeness, kindness and loyalty are the key words, not about giving money to others, let alone equality between people. Contrary to the West, where the Christian and the Enlightenment Movement have both claimed the equality between people, the Dayitong and Confucianism have both been teaching people for 2,000 years to respect and be loyal to your parents, the bosses, and the emperors. The hierarchy is a must have system. I used to look up to political leaders and the rich, and looked down on the poor, the farmers and workers, a very common attitude in China even today. The UK has taught me to see everyone as equal. I adopted this new way when I went back to China in 2019 and treated the people equally. It didn't work, because not only didn't people appreciate it, but they also abused my politeness and looked down to me. Yet they were very polite and respectful to my husband because he is white - a mad legacy left by the colonisation era. On the other hand, I have never been treated like that in the UK, because I am yellow. Due to the serious Politics Correction, Britons generally treat me equally, yet I know some of them just ignore me on purpose. I need to try harder than Britons to earn the same respect. Yet I am still happier living in the UK than in China because I can enjoy more rights and equality here, whereas in China the rights and equality or even superiority can be only bought by money and power, and not because we are all people. I shared this thought in the Chinese social media WeChat, and one of my friends said: ''I don't have money and power either, yet I don't feel I was bullied by China?'' I had no way to explain to her how equal and fair it is here, very much like when I was a kid, I didn't know how poor we were because I had no comparison.

The competition with the US has been diverted to launch the domestic social reforms, which in turn will slow down the economic progress pace. Yet it's a must-do action which will guarantee the domestic stability and progress; the priority to compete with the US.

For the US, the true enemy is not China, but the US itself. Because the last 40 years of comfortable life has been based on the exploitation of cheap labour in the third world and countries such as China, this is a fake comfort and it won't last. Furthermore, Americans care much less than the Chinese about national interest, which is the top interest providing the protection of individual rights.

Is it true that China will collapse soon? Stability overwhelms everything

In 2001, Gordon G. Chang wrote *The Coming Collapse of China*. In 2015, David Schambaugh predicted *The Coming Chinese Crack-up*. Yang Xiaokai believed China should be concerned about the Curse of the Late Comer, "a view that many developing countries failed or chose not to spend time to embrace the time-tested institutional standards and political systems. Instead, latecomers feel it is a shorter path just to mimic the advanced technologies or hardware of the system. This may eventually curb or even reverse economic growth".[6] So far these views have all failed to prove true.

Keeping domestic stability is the top issue for the Chinese government. After

Tiananmen Square, "Stability Overwhelms Everything" became a national slogan. The logic - a fast and strong economy relying on a stable society – has been very clear in everyone's mind. For people suffering from the Culture Revolution, instability will be like another nightmare. If having democracy requires another revolution, they would rather have a stable and improving life even it's not perfect. Although it's the same government that launched the Culture Revolution, overthrowing a government doing a better job now for the sake of gaining democracy is seen as not realistic or practical - the Arab Spring has shown enough examples of nations falling into dysfunction without a strong government. Dictatorship is very bad, yet it is better than chaos without security and food. Freedom sounds like a remote and beautiful dream, yet it's not that necessary. Compared to what Chinese people had –nothing during the Culture Revolution except hunger, panic and insecurity - what they are having now seems like a miracle. Financially, Chinese people can now live like the upper-middle class citizens of the West, just like the Hollywood movies show.

What do the poor in China, the true group being exploited cruelly by their Chinese and American bosses as a result of globalization, think about their life? Are they happy? I have no clue, as their voices are low and remote. Britain may still have an entrenched class system that is less explicitly defined than in previous centuries, but relative to China Britain appears a free and classless society.

It took me over one decade to get used to the strikes, protests and freedom of speech in the UK, which all looked like threatening social stability according to my former viewpoints. The United Kingdom can be dissolved through Independence Referenda, a powerful tool to separate countries, which the UK takes for granted. Yet for China, keeping its territory in full has been a holy task even at the cost of war, an unbroken idea given by Diyitong.

Chapter 2
How did America's reliance on China happen?

In the 19th Century, the British believed democracy could run capitalism best, because the debate between parties could make the best decisions for trade policy. British primitive capitalism was saved by democracy and human rights, and even the Royal family has survived so far. Two hundred years later, China is copying this and has become the world's factory. The question is how on earth a Statist country can turn into the most successful participant in global capitalism? It is because China's is a primitive style of capitalism, without the obstacles caused by human rights- an ideal land for Chinese and American businessmen.

The opportunity was given by the US first. After the Sino-Soviet split in 1966, for the sake of defeating the Soviet Union, then President Nixon visited China in 1972, which ended 25 years of no communication or diplomatic ties between the two countries. By then China was much like North Korea, a mysterious place isolated from the world.

In 1978, Deng Xiaoping made a fundamental decision to open the door to the world, because he said, "Poverty is not socialism." The Chinese government had defined China as socialist and on the way to the future of Communism where people will all have a wonderful life. I did not know China was poor until I started to watch *Gone with the Wind*, *Roman Holiday*, and other American movies in the 1980s. Then I realized that there was a different and rich world outside of my knowledge. The old western movies and old songs introduced in China shaped the impressions of generations of Chinese people about the modern west, which was another reason of why I believed that the British aristocracy was still central to British society when I came to UK in 2004.

The Beatles had little influence in China, in general. Pop music, like the Rock and Roll and Hip-hop music, are not as popular as in the West. Classical music, such as piano, opera, orchestra, has been adopted as the top-class art.

What were the viewpoints of the West regarding the Chinese economic rise?

According to Qin Hui, there are three kinds: Firstly, Chinese economic rise was a lie, and China will collapse sooner or later. The second and third one both recognized China's success, the difference being that classic liberalism believes the free market contributes to economic success, while the left wing emphasised the importance of Keynesian economics. Qin Hui's conclusion is that the low standard of human rights has been the advantage for Chinese success due to low pay and weak laws. In short, it's because that "bloody and sweat factory defeated the Western Welfare system".[1]

The three kinds of observations mentioned above about China are the typical Western perspective which, in general, fails to explain a true China as other Westerns works about China. Without understanding Dayitong and the Chinese people's mindset, Western scholars are not entitled to claim they are China experts.

Kenneth Rapoza's Forbes article helpfully describes how "In a report titled 'Invent Here, Manufacture There' published by the University of Indiana, University of Michigan professor Sridhar Kota and Thomas C. Mahoney, the associate director for MForesight, an industry think tank, wrote that U.S. dependence on foreign suppliers, and the loss of domestic suppliers, is not limited to lower cost trinkets and widgets. It runs way up the value chain, and China is key to most of it".[2]

It started from factory jobs the US gave up

The opportunity for Chinese economic progress was offered by the West, where the cost of labour had become more and more expensive. The frequent strikes and high demand of high salaries from the Unions and workers in the UK forced Thatcher to outsource labour to countries such as China in the 1980s. The whole West has enjoyed a variety of cheap goods from China for 40 years, which has now turned into a deep life dependence on China. This has finally turned into a strong confidence for China to compete with the US, as the Americans can't live without China.

China has made the most of this opportunity. The theory of the Late-mover Advantage is used by the Chinese to explain the speed of China's rise. There are more than 10 nations that have benefited from Late-mover Advantage before China including Japan, Korea, etc yet none of them can challenge the US like China today. China has received the most benefits from free trade especially after entering into the WTO.

The West believed that political reform in China would rise under a strong Chinese economy

Dependence on China was cradled by American presidents, from Bush to Clinton, and to Obama, who all believed that a strong Chinese economy would lead to a democratic China. The two key issues for China's rapid rise are the entrance to WTO and the Most Favoured Nation (MFN), offered by the Clinton government. It's the Trump administration who finally ended this naïve fantasy and turned instead to a trade war. Today The Economist has commented that "Even dovish China-watchers in America are becoming hawkish".[3]

In 2015, China's then education minister, Yuan Guiren, issued dire alarms about the threat of foreign ideas. For me, the Chinese government are over-worried about the West's influence over Chinese students. Did/will the millions of overseas Chinese students embrace the Western democracy and human rights which were/are surrounding them 24/7? I am sure the answer is very rarely because of the patriotic education they received in China. Either you love China or to love another nation, with no middle way, and yet if anyone loves other more than China then he/she is a traitor. It's just like the national identity, China doesn't allow dual nationality, if anyone would like to receive a new passport from where he/she is living, he/she has to give up the Chinese passport. It can be explained by the Confucianism which requires everyone to be loyal to the leaders, and can also be explained by the modern patriotic education, which requires the sole individual loyalty to the nation. My husband's aunt's family immigrated to Australia, holding two passports, British and Australian. They happily say they are Australian, and no one really cares about which country they love. This is almost impossible for the Chinese immigration, because China must be their Number One mother country wherever they go in the world.

The idea that Chinese students studying in the West will bring democracy back to China is naïve.

Why are the gains of American businessmen at the cost of the US? Or have Americans have had their comfortable life based on the cruel exploitation of Chinese labour?

Capitalism is the economic base for the West, but it's dangerous for climate change and national interest, and yet it's legal and right in the West under the auspices of protecting the spirit of freedom. The West has been managing the balance between the freedom of the rich and the poor, even at the cost of the national interest.

Trump started decoupling with China in the trade war of 2018 – it proved to be inefficient. It's obvious that the American businessmen investing in China have been the winners, though at the cost of the US population at large. The trade war Trump launched hasn't really stopped them from setting up factories and investing in Chinese stock markets. Why? "For all-around emerging market manufacturing know-how, for reliability, for currency stability, for safety and for domestic market growth, China is No. 1. The rest are more like No. 100", as Kenneth Rapoza argues.[4]

Decoupling from China will damage the US badly as well, according to an interview with Alexander Wyatt-Mackle, a senior economist at Oxford University on China's Global Television Network. This interview examines "how President Donald Trump's trade war with China has caused a peak loss of 245,000 U.S. jobs. Our study estimates a significant decoupling of the world's two largest economies could shrink U.S. GDP by $1.6 trillion over the next five years. This could result in 732,000 fewer U.S. jobs in 2022 and 320,000 fewer jobs by 2025. But a gradual scaling back of tariffs on both sides would boost growth and lead to an additional 145,000 jobs by 2025".[5]

Compared to Trump, Biden's government is running in a more practical way, focussing on the supply chain first. Will the claim of Xinjiang genocide stop American businessmen doing business with China? So far it hasn't happened. For American businessmen, it's profit, not the poor Chinese workers' rights, that are their concerns. After all, the majority of Americans have enjoyed decades of comfortable life by exploiting Chinese labours who are the true victims of the competition between China and the US.

Chapter 3
Why is China challenging the US now?

There has been anarchy in the international world for thousands of years, which means no true authority and international law has ever lasted as world power came and went. The only rule that has never changed is that the strongest rules.

America's rule for the last 70 years has been much more civilised than the colonization era when European countries conquered the lands and fought with each other. Nowadays the West memorized the two world wars for the sake of spirit of freedom, yet the two wars were actually the final two wars of colonisation between the world powers, in which the UK was the loser.

The American economy had bypassed the UK at the end of the 19th century, yet it refused to become a world power until the end of the second World War. Why can't China wait patiently until it has overtaken the US in GDP?

The best timing to defeat the US – The Pandemic and Capitol Hill riot

There is a popular Chinese saying – seize the historical moments. The first historical moment was the Financial Crisis in 2008, since then China started to ask for the equal relations with the US.

The year of 2020 was important for China, after it controlled Covid-19 in a relatively short time, while the US ignored the advice of the WHO and descended into a mess. The Chinese diplomatic voice became louder and stronger all of a sudden, and was suddenly described as wolf-warrior diplomacy by the West. The launch of Hong Kong security law on the 30th June 2020 shocked the West, who believed that Hong Kong is the frontline of democracy. Yet for China, "This matter is China's internal affair, and no foreign country has any right to interfere with it".[1] Hong Kong's case has shown the most serious contradiction between political and economic globalization.

The most recent historical moment for China was the Capitol Hill riot in January 2021 which shook confidence in democracy worldwide. Biden described the US Capitol riots as "one of the darkest days for our history".[2]

Will democracy in the US be defeated by internal forces? China's bet is that it will, and it's a worthy risk. After Biden had shown a tighter Chinese policy, China carried on its 'wolf-warrior' diplomacy, and in the Alaska meeting, China's top diplomat, Yang Jiechi, said that because Blinken had "delivered some quite different opening remarks, mine will be slightly different as well." He spoke for 16 minutes, blowing through the two-minute limit agreed upon in torturous pre-meeting negotiations over protocol. "Many people within the United States," he said, "actually have little confidence in the democracy of the United States." He went on to say that "China has made steady progress in human rights, and the fact is that there are many problems within the United States regarding human rights".[3]

President Xi being elected for his third term in 2022 could be one of the factors as well, because an image of China surrounded by the hostile West will speed up the need for a strong and experienced leadership in China.

He has three roles. Unlike the presidential role, which had a maximum two term limit set up by Deng Xiaoping, the two other roles of head of the Communist Party and military have no limitation of terms. In 2018, even the two-term limit for Presidency was abolished, which now implies that the Paramount leader can stay in power forever.

Xi hasn't expressed his desire for a third term. Yet the Party Central Committee in 2020 set the following long-term goals for realizing China's socialist modernization by 2035. Since the two-term limit for presidency was abolished in 2018, he is able to extend his own political ambition if he can be chosen in the 2022 by The National People's Congress. He received 100% of the vote in 2018.

China has been learning how to rule the world

From 2002 to 2013 while Hu Jintao was in the power, over 140 professors and scholars from universities and institutions were invited to give lectures about the history of the communist party, SARS, how to improve the administration ability of the communist party, etc... to the members of Politburo of the Chinese Communist Party in Zhongnanhai, the political centre of China.

One special lecture was titled *The Rise of the Great Powers*, a 12-part Chinese documentary television series produced by CCTV and broadcast in 2006. The leaders studied nine world powers' rise including Portugal, Spain, the Netherlands, the UK, France, Germany, Japan, Russia (Soviet Union), and the US.

Wang Huning is now in the top 5 of the Politburo Standing Committee, and is Xi's close advisor, with professional knowledge about International relations and politics. He serviced three Chinese leaders from Jiang Zeming, Hu Jingtao and Xi, was believed to be the master of Xi's idea of the "Chinese Dream" and "Xi Jinping Thought" ideologies.

Wang Huning is the author of *America against America*, published in China in 1991 after he, then a Chinese scholar, finished visiting the US, in which he writes "In general, the American system is based on individual interest, Hedonism and democracy, obviously, it's defeated by a collective, Altruism and Authoritarianism system (in Japan)".[4] His judgements have been put into practice for three decades – China is competing with the American system by using their system of 'Chinese collective'; Altruism and Authoritarianism.

In terms of war, by learning from the US's costly involvement in Iraq, Afghanistan, etc, China has adopted the policy of non-alignment. The US has finally recognized the problems from its former foreign policy. In 2021, Blinken said: "as the President has promised, diplomacy – not military action – will always come first. Again, this is shaped by hard lessons learned. Americans are rightly wary of prolonged U.S. military interventions abroad. We've seen how they've often come at far too high a cost, both to us and to others. When we look back at the past decades of our military involvement in the world, especially in Afghanistan and the Middle East, we must remember what we've learned about the limits of force to build a durable peace; that the day after a major military intervention is always harder than we imagine; and how critical it is to pursue every possible avenue to a diplomatic solution".[5]

Despite domestic and international criticism, Biden withdrew the army from Afghanistan by the end of August 2021. He said he needed to face the current threat, not the old one. Who are the current threats? He means Russian and China.

The US will defeat itself through its own businessmen

The Western system is people oriented, so people, not the country as a gestalt, has been the core of America. Yet a policy which pleases the majority of people isn't necessarily the best one for the national power. On the contrary, sometimes it can be at the cost of the national power, which is the foundation for global reputation.

While all 1.3 billion Chinese citizens are aware of the competition between US and China, only very few British people are able to understand the ongoing fight. I was very surprised to figure out that the British have not much interest in world politics, as the domestic TV and media mostly focus on domestic issues, while the Chinese state media show global political issues to people every day.

Chinese people are used to boycotting any product produced from an unfriendly nation. Supported by the government and state media, the boycott itself has been taken as a patriotic movement. For instance, CNN reported "H&M and Nike are facing a boycott in China over Xinjiang cotton statements".[6]

There is nothing like this in the US, because the behaviour of businesses and customers are free from politics. Nowadays, even after the Biden government has taken China as its only strong competitor, Americans still love to buy Made-in-China products, as businessmen have still taken China as the best country in which to invest.

The Biden government have been trying to unite the whole west in the name of protecting human rights and world order, but so far it hasn't affected the economic movement. Joe McDonald wrote in the Diplomat that "for the first three months of 2021, [Chinese] exports jumped 49 percent over a year earlier to $710 billion. Imports rose 28 percent to $593.6 billion".[7]

David Goldman reported on CNN: "2020 marked the first year in history that foreign direct investment in China overtook that of the US, according to the UN. China is now the world's largest recipient of foreign companies' investments."[8]

Chinese national interests have been in line with individual interest twice - getting rich and achieving collective security in the pandemic

Autocracy has been described as a bad system, in which politics is an issue only reserved for the government. Yet for China, where people had nothing before the 1978, every improvement was and is taken as progress by its people. Food and security are overwhelmingly more important than freedom of speech, free media, and the ability to protest, a feeling that relatively few in the US can comprehend.

The strong, singular, and long-term collective priority has been the Chinese communist party, which controls all of the national resources including finance, land, and media. Though the party suffered during the Cultural Revolution, it is going from strength to strength in the 21st century. This has resulted from China's economic rise amid the Pandemic battle, due to its exclusive match with Chinese people's needs, which put the individual and national interest in the same path and direction.

For over 2,000 years, China was under the control of Dayitong, an Imperial system which ran in the same way throughout – a strong government, and obedient people who looked up to the government and the police force. The Communist Party has carried on this way by blocking Western websites, news, and all of the Western social media - the easiest and most primitive governing approach. I have experienced a totally different world from China after emigrating to the UK in 2004. My Chinese friends failed to notice it and carried on talking to me with Chinese logic, as they have no clue what I have seen in the West. Meanwhile, I have no way to make them understand British societies where the poor, the disabled, other minorities, and even the prisoners are treated so well.

Entrepreneurs have become the biggest star in China. Getting richer and richer in a highly competitive environment is a virtue

When the slogan, 'the first cat to catch the rat is the best cat, no matter black cat or white cat', was put forth by Deng Xiaoping in the 1980s, people loved it. The Chinese were so poor that they therefore had no fear - what could they lose? The cat theory sounded so encouraging: if you work hard, at least you can have a bit of a better life. I myself had no idea of the impact of laws, inequality, human rights, and racism, all of which only made sense to me after I went to the UK.

'Time is money, the efficiency is the Life' was another popular slogan in the 1980s.

To achieve something important is the only goal in the life; otherwise you are wasting your life. To be relaxed, to be laid back, to enjoy time passing, are all sinful. I did not have any idea of 'holidays' before I was 18 years old, when the Ten-thousand-yuan household (people getting rich by hard work with about £1,300 in the bank) had become a new and admiring word - then the numbers of millionaires increased rapidly. Millionaires quickly became billionaires after I came to the UK. China doesn't allow dual citizenships, so many of the UK Chinese population keep their Chinese passports in case they go back to China one day to make more money.

China, after I left, has become more and more competitive. When I was a poor child in the 1970s and 1980s, I did not know the world. I was actually OK, not having much homework and pressure. Nowadays, after the One Child Policy has been cancelled, some Chinese women refuse to have a second child due to the fierce competition of social status and costly education fees. For women without a wealthy family background, rising to the top of the social ladder requires either hard work with a lot of luck, marrying a rich man, or expecting your child to be successful. This is because people's success in China is judged not only by their personal achievement, but also the achievement of their children. 'Every parent expects their kids to be a dragon' is an old Chinese saying, as the image of the Dragon used to be only reserved for Chinese emperors. How does one turn a child into a dragon? By education. This principle even holds for the rich and powerful families. For a Chinese child, competition starts from 4 years old. The child has to learn everything: academic works; English; piano; violin; drawing and more. The meaning of life is to win this competition, not to explore who you are and what you want to do. Getting into the top Universities (Oxford, Harvard, etc.) has been the collective dream for Chinese tiger parents who put high pressure and hopes on their children. This kind of tough parenting style is taken as love, care, and responsibility, but will these days be seen as harmful to the mental health of children by Western standards.

I turned into a British-style mother after having been a tiger mother for three years. My transformation was really hard. At the beginning I felt guilty as I felt like I wasn't a good mother, and was failing to fulfil my parental duties. I may be one of the first few Chinese immigrant parents who are aware and willing to transfer, as the majority of British Chinese parents still practise the Chinese method.

Individual duties come first

I don't know how many Westerners understand this Chinese logic that without the protection that China affords, it would be impossible for any Chinese individual to survive. Therefore, it is a civic duty to put national interest ahead of any individual interest, as the reverse would be selfish. In the four years since Brexit, and the more than one year battle against Covid-19 in the UK, what I have seen is the absence of the spirit of protecting national benefit, of a sense of collective security, and of individual duties.

In general, there are five kinds of interests and duties for a country: individual, community, party, government, and national. In China, only national interest and individual duties matter, there is next to no conflict between different groups of interests, or if there is then such conflict can be hidden. The Womb's Vote mentioned before was the best example.

In the West, individual interests often come first, party interests second, and national interest last. In terms of duties, the government carries the burden, with individuals having far fewer. During Brexit individual and party interest were both in conflict with national interest, and it took almost four years for the UK to find a way out as MPs only cared about their party interests, meaning national interest was ultimately sacrificed.

The Pandemic has been very much like war time, when all people's interests are supposed to unite together due to the common enemy: the virus. The most efficient way to defeat the virus is to put all of the interests and duties across all groups, from individual to the government, together. The Chinese knew this from the beginning, and stood with the government unconditionally, secured by the strong forces of the policemen. Yet in the UK, individual interests have been the priority.

The fact that protecting the country *equals* protecting individuals was missed. Perhaps some people mixed up national interest with the Conservative party's interest and tried their best to keep their human rights and freedom in case they were taken away by the government (who were actually trying to save the nation). In general, all kinds of interest have been in conflict during the pandemic, which results in long term pain and costly debt for the nation.

Social media has done a bad job by spreading lies, yet this is tolerated by the UK and US government. So far there are no serious laws to control social media because of the strong tradition of freedom of speech.

If China goes to one extreme, where it mainly cares about national rights/interests and personal duties, then the West goes to the other extreme by mainly caring about individual rights of the voters and governmental duties, where national interest is sometimes neglected.

The Difference between the British and the Chinese

Biden criticized Chinese President Xi Jinping for not having "a democratic bone in his body," which may resonate in the West, yet rarely hurts the Chinese, who have no true idea of democracy and human rights.

Educated by the free media and state-run media separately, Americans and the Chinese observe things from the following opposite directions:

Attitude to the world: Chinese people believe they are living in a world where China has been bullied by the West, where they have to fight due to the strong belief of Social Darwinism domestically and internationally. Americans believe they live in a society with peace and safety, protected by the US government which rules the world.

Attitude to government: The Chinese are obedient, while Americans are sceptical.

Attitude to national leader: The Chinese believe their leader is strong, kind, and fair - they are sometimes even seen as a God-figure. Americans believe their leader has to be watched carefully otherwise corruption will happen.

Attitude to work: Chinese people work much harder than Americans due to the absence of protection by a welfare system, and severe competition among citizens.

Attitude to life: Encouraged by the government, Chinese people prefer to make the most of every minute to earn money or to be higher and higher in the social hierarchy. The saying, 'enjoy happiness when you suffer from hard study or work', shows that Chinese life is a competition with their fellow people, while Americans believe in hedonism.

Attitude to tolerance: The Chinese are highly tolerant of hardship, unfairness, inequality, and indignity. I didn't understand the severity of this slave spirit in China until I moved to the UK.

Attitude to death: the majority of Chinese people have no belief in the afterlife, so being dead is a cold and lonely ending. The Chinese try to distance themselves from the dead. The tombs in China are built in remote places, meaning tombs in churches are a horrifying scene for Chinese people, who will feel they are dying soon. The belief that a life without quality is better than being dead has been highly popular in China. It is this which made civilians more aware of the threat of Covid-19, kept them indoors, and prevented its spread. My Chinese friends refused to go out even after China had suppressed the virus in the middle of 2020. The government in fact had to encourage them to get out to revive the economy.

What are the strategies for the US and China in this race?

The US strategy – political globalization first, free trade second

Trump's China policy was a rash and impractical one, hoping to decouple from China as soon as possible. Biden has learned the lesson; he now focuses on protecting the most important American supply chains first. The White House issued the Executive Order on America's Supply Chains on the 24th Feb 2021.

In terms of policy left from the trade war, the New York Times reported: "The hard choices for Mr. Biden will include deciding whether to maintain tariffs on about $360 billion worth of Chinese imports, which have raised costs for American businesses and consumers".[9]

Will Biden bar the investments in Chinese firms with military ties? According to a report on the 6th of May 2021 by Bloomberg, "Biden Team [is] Likely to Proceed With Trump China Investment Ban".[10]

On the 18th May 2021, voted through 86-11, the Endless Frontier Act was opened for debated in The U.S. Senate. "The Endless Frontier Act would authorize most of the money, $100 billion, to invest in basic and advanced research, commercialization of the research, and education and training programs in key technology areas like artificial intelligence (AI)".[11]

Senate Majority Leader Chuck Schumer said: "We can either have a world where the Chinese Communist Party determines the rules of the road for 5G, artificial intelligence and quantum computing — or we can make sure the United States gets there first."[12]

In terms of how to stop the economic movement of American businessmen, it looks like the discovery of Xinjiang internment camps, national security, and even the origin of Covid-19 are all going to play a significant role for the future - creating a wider awareness of political correctness and ethical responsibility in the West to self-censor American consumers and businessmen.

Chinese strategy – the strongest promoter of economic globalization, yet preparing for exclusively domestic business

China had hoped for a less tense relationship with the Biden government. Knowing this would be impossible, however, China has determined to go on its own way, and has prepared for the worst-case scenario: Biden successfully stopping Western reliance on China.

China launched the dual circulation policy in May 2020, which will carry on developing the economy on two levels:

domestic and international economic movement. Reuters explains how "Chinese President Xi Jinping first raised the idea in May and later elaborated that China will rely mainly on 'internal circulation' - the domestic cycle of production, distribution, and consumption - for its development, supported by innovation and upgrades in the economy. Xi also said 'internal circulation' will be supported by 'external circulation'".[13]

So far, Biden's government has allied with the UK, Canada, Australia, and even the EU has started to trust the US after the four years of Trump's government. China used to hope to keep positive relations with the EU, yet the frozen Comprehensive Agreement on Investment put the permissive future for Sino-EU relations on hold.[14]

Relations between China has Russia are at an all-time high. Just a few days after the Alaska meeting, the foreign ministers of the two sides met. On the 24th May 2021, Chinese top diplomat Yang Jieci visited Russia for a new round of strategic security consultation. Yang Sheng reported in the

Global Times: "Frequent interactions between Beijing and Moscow show great mutual-trust and interdependency. These interactions are necessary amid the rising pressure and hostility from the US […] The upcoming China-Russia meeting will take place just a few days after the top leaders of the two countries witnessed the ground-breaking of key cooperative nuclear energy projects last week."[15]

In terms of being the global leader of AI, Indermit Gill commented:

"In 2015, it (China) announced the $1.68 trillion Made in China 2025 plan, to do with artificial intelligence what Lenin had done for electric power. The plan is to transform the Chinese economy and dominate global manufacturing by 2030".[16]

Chapter 4

How did the misunderstanding between China and the West happen?

After having written for about 10 years about British society, culture, and politics for Financial Times Chinese readers, I realized that China and the UK have almost nothing in common. They are bound to misunderstand everything except trade and business. One Chinese officer was not happy with my opinion in 2019, when China was still keen to be closer to the West and tried very hard to show an image of Chinese civilization. The officer felt that my views showed their hard work – trying to bridge the West and China – didn't go down well. My opinions sounded like a criticism of their work. Yet only few people like me, who were born, grew up, educated, and worked in China before emigrating to the West, are able to really see through the difference between China and the West. I felt I was educated, fashionable, civilized and modern before I came to the UK. I soon realized I was so wrong once I'd lived in the UK and deeply understood it – my brain was just like a granny, very old fashioned compared to British modern standards. Even the British private educational system is unfair, and yet the Chinese educational system is even worse. There are about 93% of students in state schools all experiencing the same teaching quality, China's hierarchical educational system means living and learning in a tough and severe competitive environment. Whilst below them are the poor farmers' children who only have the basic educational opportunities. And at the top are a small number of the kids from the elite families in Beijing who embrace the best educational resources, and the middle group are the Wombs Vote's power who suffer enough. Can any Westerners living in China compare China and the West well and with a deep understanding? I'm not sure.

Before China became determined to follow its own path in 2021, it had been trying very hard to shape the Chinese image in the world. 'To tell the Chinese story well in the world' has been an important job for the government. Considerable amounts of money have been spent of it by means of newspaper, TV, social media for decades. It all failed. Why? Because China can't understand the modern West and has been trying to shape its image according to its own Chinese method, which is either old fashioned or too Chinese. The Chinese effort of trying to be understood by the West has never been appreciated by the West, which was a shame. Otherwise, the competition between China and the US could have been less of a conflict.

Why can't the West understand China?

Because the West, especially the US, is too young, too strong and too advanced, unable to devote time for understanding the history before the US and UK were born, and keen to save the world by its own way.

Trade has been the main theme throughout the human history, whoever ran the country, however cruel the leader was, no one can stop the eagerness and enthusiasm of businessmen. It has run in parallel with wars and peace, and the highest form of trade is capitalism via the economic globalization, in which China is the latest and strongest promoter succeeding the US and the West, and has become the most desirable territory for the Western businessmen and consumers, who don't have much moral obligation and duty for their own nations.

The tradition of free trade was introduced by British empire in the early 19th century, which was keen to do trade with the whole world. China Qing dynasty, an old and rich nation getting used to self-sufficiency and one with no interest in trade, became one of the victims of

British colonization policy, especially after the Opium War in 1839, when the British empire was keen to extend the market and sell the opium in China. It was taken for granted due to the anarchic principle in the international world; if a nation is weak and poor, it deserved to be bullied or even destroyed.

For almost 200 years China, which used to be proud of its own advanced culture, was regarded as a poor and weak nation. For the last 70 years it had another image in the West; 'the Communism country'. For the most recent 40 years, it has been taken as world factory providing cheap products, its new role in the world. The books in the West market told how to do business with Chinese and the sad Chinese stories in the Cultural Revolution have been popular. Few books and articles really noticed the pain China suffered from the Opium War, the China's national emotion about the revival of Chinese glory, let alone the 2,000 years history of Dayitong system.

China shocked the world when it made it clear it was not going to follow American policy anymore and was determined to go its own way. How can China turn against us when we have given so much help to it? Some politician felt sad. Since the US launched the human rights foreign policy from the time of the

Carter government, the entire West have felt they are saving the world, a very justified action, which has been accepted and supported by every individual, media, political party, and governments.

Four questions have never got into the Westerner's mind:

1. can the West last forever?
2. are you supporting your own competitor who may take over your market position?
3. How many people realize that enjoying the 'Made in China' products is against the spirit of Human rights and contributing to more pressure on climate change? The theory of Competitive Advantage doesn't suit in this area.
4. Western history has shown that the lower-class people who were bullied would definitely fight and become equal with the formal powerful class, by violence, peaceful democracy, or other methods. What do you think China will do in the future when Chinese are more powerful? They will ask for equality and fairness like any Western working class had done. Actually, they are doing now.

Very few Westerners will worry about the fate of their own nations. Even if democracy dies, surely the countries can still survive? For the

US, it's too early to worry as it is still the king in the world. Also, it's too young, less than 300 hundred years old, not old enough to experience the bitter taste of being bullied, occupied or destroyed. For the UK, the formal empire, it has been an old monarchy lasting for almost 1,000 years from the William Conqueror, the ancestor of the Queen of Elizabeth II. When many other European monarchies died in the 19th century, the British monarchy survived by democracy resulting from the Enlightenment Movement, the Glorious Revolution, the Magna Carta, and so on. The only pain of scale the whole nation remembers was the danger when Hitler tried to dominate Europe.

It's freedom that was highlighted. What does freedom mean? I think it means individual freedom, not national freedom, not least the demise of the UK, because the UK has never really died like China did. That's why Britons have no idea about defending the fate of nation until their own individual freedom is challenged collectively. What kinds of circumstance would the Brits need to defend the fate of the UK? Only military war, not trade war, nor Covid-19.

China has died many times, not by invasion, but mainly by its domestic collapse due to the rebellion of poor peasants who had no hope for life. China is a general name for the dynasties from different families controlling relatively the same territories, whether larger or smaller, as is the case in China today. They run the nation by Han people, speaking and writing the same languages, Han language, worshiping the same value of Confucianism, adopting the Dayitong political method. The main dynasties were:

Qin dynasty (BC221 – BC206, 15 years),

West Han dynasty (BC202 – AD 8, 210 years),

Dong Han dynasty (AD 25 -220, 195years),

Tang dynasty (618 -907, 289 years),

North Song dynasty (960 – 1127, 167year),

South Song dynasty (1127 – 1279, 152years),

Yuan dynasty (1271 – 1368, 97 years),

Ming dynasty (1368 – 1644, 276 years),

Qing dynasty (1644 – 1912 268 years),

They are different from British dynasties, which have blood links between them. Chinese Emperors in different dynasties were from different families.

China's history has been really unique compared to the Middle East and Europe.

Geographically, China is located at the far east end of the Eurasia, the origins of the main civilizations before the US was born. Before the aeroplane was invented, the communication and trade in the Eurasia had been regional, it's rare to see references about the British empire, on the other side of the Eurasia, an island, in Chinese early history record.

This contrasts with the land in the middle part of the Eurasia, say the Middle East and Europe, where the owners changed now and then due to the frequent wars. For example, Constantinople, the former capital of Byzantine Empire, was conquered by The Ottoman Empire in 1453. Baghdad, the capital of Iraq, was founded by the Abbasid Caliphate in the 8th century, and controlled by Mongolia, Persia, and The Ottoman Empire historically. Thanks to its geographic location, China had been a relative stable position, as its east side is the sea, and the South-west side is The Himalayas, both of which provide national protection. Before the British empire launched the Opium war, the biggest enemy for China was Mongolia which controlled China for 97 years, because they had adopted the Chinese language, Dayitong bureaucracy, and values to manage the land and people. This 97 years of dominant control by foreigners, not Han people, the major ethnic of China, was and is seen as a key part of Chinese history.

Although the majority of Chinese dynasties were run by Han people, they were from different families and backgrounds - nobles, farmers, military force, etc. It's a common sense in China that Chinese dynasties came and went, no one lasted for over 300 years, yet Chinese culture has never died. Because after one dies, a new one would be rebuilt in much the same way with the Dayitong bureaucracy and values just like Mongolia did.

For a very long time, Chinese wondered why the Britain can evolve so quick and so well, from a barbarian place to the most advanced nation in less than 1,000 years, yet China has been repeated its cycle and hasn't really changed much for 2,000 years?

Jin Guantao and Liu Qingfeng explained the reason very well in The Cycle of Growth and Decline On the Ultrastable Structure of Chinese Society1. In general, they believe that there are four essential elements in the cycle of 2,000 years:

1. The Dayitong set by emperor Qin Shi Huang who standardized the money, measurement methods and language before BC206,

2. Confucianism was set as the only value and religion by Dong Zhongshu (179–104 BC) in West Han dynasty, which requires everyone to be loyal to the father, husband, and emperor. It also positioned the Emperor as the only holy person sent from the heaven. "At the same time, as Confucians, the educated firmly supported the rites of ancestor worship, the traditional beliefs associated with those rites, and the claims of the Emperor to be the mediating priest between Heaven and Earth'.

3. Shi, the Chinese Intellectuals, who took the Dayitong and Confucianism as the only true belief, and played a key role to build the new dynasty.

4. The patriarchal system on two levels: national level and family level. The latter carried the gene of patriarchal system of national level when the dynasty collapse, and grow into a new one.

5. The agricultural economy - land was the main source of income.

According to Jin Guantao and Liu Qingfeng, the cycle was: a new dynasty was built and turned rich and strong, the corruption and annexation of land finally exploited peasants to such an extreme and the only hope was to rail against the landlord and local governments. Then the whole dynasty turned into turmoil, with the help from the patriarchal system at family level, the gene of how to organize a dynasty well, and the Shi people who knew how to organize. There were three endings:

1. The leading rebellion peasant became the new emperor, example; Emperor Gaozu of Han (Liu Bang) in the West Han dynasty (BC202 – AD 8) and The Hongwu Emperor (Zhu Yuanzhang) in Ming dynasty (1368 – 1644).

2. The chaos was used by some noble families to fight for the top position and become the new emperor, examples of which are, Emperor Gaozu of Tang in Tang dynasty (618 -907), Emperor Taizu of Song in North Song dynasty (960 – 1127)

3. The minority took advantage of the chaos and set up a new dynasty, say China's final dynasty - Qing dynasty (1644 – 1912).

Why did the dynasties repeat the same way, with only a little amount of reform or change? Because this Chinese system had been proved to be effective in carrying the reborn Gene. Also, it had been more advanced than other cultures nearby, so the Yuan and Qing dynasty who were not Han people, had to adopt this method to rule China.

Why didn't it evolve like British society? Because Dayitong system required strong, tight and dominating control to the society to preserve the superiority of the emperors, it didn't leave much room for new things to grow and develop.

This system had been effective until the British Empire started the free trade with its guns and canons. Since then, Chinese have been trying to copy science, military and democracy from the West, which all failed until the People's Republic of China (1949-present) introduced state capitalism, which led to the miracle – China turned into the second place in GDP after the US. Why didn't China introduce capitalism before? Because businessmen had been in the lowest position in Chinese society where the agricultural economics had been the king and protected by the whole system. Also, Chinese state capitalism didn't work until the price of labour in the West reached higher and higher.

Why doesn't the West know the Chinese pain and anger to the West due to the Opium War? There are two reasons:

1. China has rarely mentioned the Opium War in its foreign policy and condemned the wrongdoing of the Opium War in public. No one knows why.
2. British society has stopped mentioning the Opium War since the early 20th century. Only a few books, radio programs, and documentaries about this war are available in the UK. I launched the campaign of putting Opium War in school curriculum in 2019, and received the support from Ken Hom, Lord Goldsmith, Sir Vince Cable, Sir Martin Sorrel, Dan Snow and Lord Pendry. Nick Gibb, the Minister of State at the Department for Education, sent a formal reply[4] to me saying 'No'. The Xinhua News Agency, the official state-run press agency of the People's Republic of China and the biggest and most influential media organization in China, reported the news of this campaign – *British Chinese Scholar Calls for the Opium War to be Included in the British Secondary School History Curriculum*[3] – and which was reported by hundreds of Chinese media afterwards.

Why can't China understand the West?

Although Chinese culture has been long and rich, it has no way of understanding a new value based on individual interest. Fairness, equality, protest, freedom of speech, and so on are all attractive but alien as well.

The era of Britain Feudal system before the Glory Revolution in 1688, was similar to the Chinese Feudal system before Qin Shihuang which defeated six other nations and united the seven nations to become one country – Qin dynasty (BC221 – BC206). And this was more than 1,000 years earlier than European Feudal system. The Chinese feudal system went into Dayitong since BC221, yet the British feudal system transitioned into democracy from 1688, in which the power sharing from the King to the aristocracy, to rich middle-class men, to all men and women, to people of different races. The privileges of the King and aristocracy were depleted. The monarchy survived but at the cost of their freedom of speech - giving up their political power and keeping quiet about any political opinions. The fate of aristocracy is not much better than that – they lost their political power, the guardian of their land and wealth.

China has stayed at a primitive stage for over 2,000 years – the power has only been in the hands of emperors, now, of the Supreme leader Xi. Power sharing has rarely happened in Chinese history, occasionally only with the PMs. Although the new concepts of democracy, freedom, liberty, fairness, and so on were introduced into China from the 19th century, what the Chinese really know well is Marxism, socialism, reviving China's glory, defending China, never forgetting Chinese national humiliation, patriotic spirit, etc. That's why almost no one in Mainland China felt sorry for Hong Kong people when the Security Law was introduced in 2020, as they have no sense of freedom and liberty, concepts which are too advanced and too far from Chinese life.

In the summer of 2021, Xi presented the idea of common prosperity, one of the legacies left by Deng Xiaoping who led China open to capitalism, a very brave move under a tense Chinese atmosphere set against market and capital. The common prosperity is a new task which has never happened before. Sharing money with the poor means less strength to compete with the US, so why did Xi proposed this idea only a few months after China made it clear it was intending to go its own way? Some media said it's the government's plan. That's true but I think the reason why the common prosperity was sped up was because of the *Wombs Vote*, and the government knew it had to push people to very extreme levels for the last four decades, fairness reform has to start without any delay. Yet, compared to the West society, where people are spoilt according to the Chinese perspective, China has just started its first step on the way to fairness, which is the most distinctive approach from all prior dynasties and may lay an important foundation for a longer life of the domination of the Chinese Communist Party.

Chapter 5
Conclusion

Is capitalism the must have economic style we have to embrace?

Will climate change turn the direction of capitalism?

Are democracy and welfare systems the only political method to compromise capitalism?

Can China find out a new way to manage capitalism, and keep domestic stability for the long term?

There are many uncertain issues ahead of us. The ongoing competition between China and the US may contribute to offer the answers at the end. In general, this is a historical repetition of competition between world powers, now at a higher scientific and more environmental level.

Specifically, there are four points worth remembering. First is the problematic legacy leftover from colonization. Seeking the right for racial national pride is a Chinese version of BLM on the international level. The co-existence of the US welfare system and the business profits derived from exploiting cheaper labours in China shows that the USA's human rights foreign policy is boneless.

Secondly, a sense of collective security, or personal duty is missing in the US. Compared to the Chinese, who believe that they are surrounded by internal and external troubles, and that working and fighting hard is the only way out, Americans have been living in a safe zone since the US established its global cultural hegemony after the Cold War. Perhaps the common sense of this obligation of collective security can be roused in wartime, not in a Pandemic, let alone the competition with China.

For Chinese people, Covid-19 is just like a war zone. From the beginning, Chinese people knew very soon that the right thing to do was to wear a facemask, keep socially distanced, and stay at home - all of which took a much longer time to happen in the UK. This is because British people don't trust the suggestions of their government, have less fear about the virus, and can't bear to stay at home. The realisation that normality would return if everyone sacrificed their own individual interests for a short time for the sake of collective benefit was/is quite absent. China made it happen in one month, the UK took more than one year.

Ignorance of this national level of collective interest is dangerous, because it is the nation, not individual, that is the basic unit in the international world. It's national power that provides the foundation to individual interests when a common enemy appears.

Thirdly, compared to autocracy, democracy and human rights are the best way for domestic peace, fairness, and equality. Yet, in terms of international relations, political/cultural hegemony has been the norm - a long term unsorted problem for the history of mankind. The US has been trying to rule the world with foreign policy which preaches human rights yet also practises violence, and China is striving for equality in the name of sovereignty.

Human history has shown that autocracy never lasts, but it can be very strong and powerful for decades, even hundreds of years. The voting system has brought domestic peace in liberal democratic countries, yet the worrying problems of liberal democracy are the collapse of the middle-class voters, and the uncontrollable greed of capitalism - take, for example, the Great Depression, or the 2008 Financial Crisis, where businessmen's gains were at the cost of the US's interest as a nation. So far, the fate of liberal democracy has been too young to predict.

In terms of global competition, Biden said that "Everyone must play by the same rules".[1] The Chinese government said that China only wants to "surpass ourselves for a better China, so that our people will enjoy a better life",[2] and that "China's goal has never been to surpass U.S".[3] Whatever they say, it's a historical competition, with one winner, one loser.

Finally, it's a competition at the cost of economic globalization or democracy. Can the full scale of globalization come back to what it was before 2016? In the short term, no. If China wins, economic globalization wins and democracy loses. If the US wins, it will be the opposite. Yet in the long term the answer is as Martin Wolf predicted: "yes. It requires peace among the great powers. Some would also argue it requires a hegemonic power, like the UK before 1914 and the US after 1945".[4] So, will it be the US, China, or any other new unexpected world power? Wait and see.

Endnotes

Introduction

1. "600 million people whose monthly income was barely 1,000 yuan ($154)": BBC, https://www.bbc.co.uk/news/56213271

2. "Red Army soldiers stayed fearless": China.org, http://www.china.org.cn/china/2021-04/26/content_77442026.htm

Chapter 1

1. "China believes that it-- it-- it can be and should be and will be the dominant-- country in the world": CBS, https://www.cbsnews.com/news/antony-blinken-60-minutes-2021-05-02/

2. "Due to the Correct Chinese Political Approach, We Have Been Overtaking the UK and US": Xinhuanet, http://www.xinhuanet.com/politics/2015-10/19/c_128335233.htm

3. "this group of people gathered together last time was in 1900, 120 years have passed, they are still dreaming to (bully us)": Xinhuanet, http://www.xinhuanet.com/world/2021-05/09/c_1211147404.htm

4. "The Planned economy doesn't mean socialism": Gov.cn, http://www.gov.cn/jrzg/2009-09/24/content_1425253.htm

5. "Human rights are also co-equal": USA TODAY, https://eu.usatoday.com/story/news/politics/2021/03/30/antony-blinken-slams-trumps-hierarchy-human-rights-skewed/4805345001/

6. "a view that many developing countries failed": sec.gov, https://www.sec.gov/comments/emerging-markets/cll9-7418355-219651.htm

Chapter 2

1. "bloody and sweat factory defeated the Western Welfare system": Aisixiang website, https://www.aisixiang.com/data/11061.html

2. "In a report titled "Invent Here, Manufacture There": Forbes, https://www.forbes.com/sites/kenrapoza/2020/04/30/why-is-the-us-is-so-ridiculously-dependent-on-china/?sh=77a4af2656b5

3. "Even dovish China-watchers in America are becoming hawkish": The Economist, https://www.economist.com/china/2021/05/01/even-doveish-china-watchers-in-america-are-becoming-hawkish?fsrc=rss

4. "For all-around emerging market manufacturing": Forbes, https://www.forbes.com/sites/kenrapoza/2019/09/03/why-american-companies-choose-china-over-everyone-else/?sh=1b8b5a0371de

5. "how President Donald Trump's trade war with China": Oxford economics, http://blog.oxfordeconomics.com/trumps-trade-war-with-china-has-cost-us-jobs

Chapter 3

1. "This matter is China's internal affair and no foreign country has any right to interfere with it": Chinese Ministry of Foreign Affairs Website

https://www.fmprc.gov.cn/mfa_eng/xwfw_665399/s2510_665401/2511_665403/t1784166.shtml

2. "one of the darkest days for our history": Daily telegraph, https://www.telegraph.co.uk/news/2021/01/07/congress-riots-senate-georgia-result-donald-trump-capitol-latest/

3. "Many people within the United States": Brookings website https://www.brookings.edu/blog/order-from-chaos/2021/03/22/the-us-and-china-finally-get-real-with-each-other/

4. "In general, the American system is based on individual interest": 163 news website, https://www.163.com/dy/article/E44LQUBI05416I4C.html

5. "as the President has promised, diplomacy – not military action": US State website, https://www.state.gov/a-foreign-policy-for-the-american-people/

6. ''H&M and Nike are facing a boycott in China over Xinjiang cotton statements'': CNN, https://edition.cnn.com/2021/03/25/business/hm-nike-xinjiang-cotton-boycott-intl-hnk/index.html

7. "For the first three months of 2021": Diplomat website https://thediplomat.com/2021/04/chinas-exports-rise-as-global-demand-revives/#:~:text=Exports%20rose%20to%20%24241.1%20billion,sign%20of%20reviving

8. "2020 marked the first year in history": CNN, https://edition.cnn.com/2021/01/24/investing/us-china-foreign-direct-investment/index.html

9. "The hard choices for Mr. Biden will include deciding": New York Times, https://www.nytimes.com/2020/11/16/business/economy/biden-china-trade-policy.html

10. " Biden Team Likely to Proceed With Trump China Investment Ban": Bloomberg, https://www.bloomberg.com/news/articles/2021-05-06/biden-team-likely-to-proceed-on-trump-s-china-investment-ban

11. "The Endless Frontier Act would authorize most of the money, $100 billion": Reuters, https://www.reuters.com/technology/us-senate-votes-open-debate-china-tech-bill-2021-05-17/

12. "We can either have a world where the Chinese Communist Party ": Politico, https://www.politico.com/news/2021/05/17/senate-bipartisan-deal-countering-china-489152

13. "'internal circulation' will be supported by 'external circulation'": Reuters, https://www.reuters.com/article/china-economy-transformation-explainer-idUSKBN2600B5

14. "MEPs vote to freeze controversial EU-China investment deal": Euronews, https://www.euronews.com/2021/05/20/european-parliament-votes-to-freeze-controversial-eu-china-investment-deal

15. "Frequent interactions between Beijing and Moscow show great mutual-trust ": Global Times, https://www.globaltimes.cn/page/202105/1224261.shtml

16. "In 2015, it (China) announced the $1.68 trillion Made in China 2025 plan": Brookings website, https://www.brookings.edu/blog/future-development/2020/01/17/whoever-leads-in-artificial-intelligence-in-2030-will-rule-the-world-until-2100/

Chapter 4

1, Jin Guantao and Liu Qingfeng. The Cycle of Growth and Decline On the Ultrastable Structure of Chinese Society, Law Press China, 2010

2, C.P.Fitzgerald. The Chinese View of their Place in the World, Oxford University Press, 1964

3, *British Chinese scholar calls for the Opium War to be included in the British secondary school history curriculum*: Xinhuanet, http://www.xinhuanet.com/world/2019-05/10/c_1124479157.htm

2019-0016950POGibb

Rt Hon Nick Gibb MP
Minister of State for School Standards

Sanctuary Buildings, 20 Great Smith Street, Westminster, London, SW1P 3BT
tel: 0370 000 2288 www.education.gov.uk/help/contactus

Mr Zac Goldsmith MP
By email: zac@zacgoldsmith.com

15 May 2019

Dear Zac

Thank you for your email of 28 April, addressed to the Secretary of State, enclosing correspondence from your constituent, Mrs Yue Parkinson, regarding history education. I am replying as the Minister of State for School Standards.

History is a compulsory subject in the National Curriculum for pupils aged 5-14. The history curriculum sets out, within a chronological framework, the core knowledge that enables pupils to understand the history of Britain from its first settlers to the development of the institutions that help to define our national life today, as well as aspects of European and wider world history. It does not set out every event, person or institution that pupils should be taught about, and there is flexibility for a range of different approaches. Teachers have the freedom to teach lessons that are right for their pupils and should use teaching materials that suit their pupils' needs. The teaching of any issue in schools should be consistent with the principles of balance and objectivity.

The history curriculum, which sets out mandatory themes that maintained schools in England must cover, is available at: tinyurl.com/Pbl7ePh.

In order to provide a period of stability to schools, the Secretary of State has committed to making no new changes to the National Curriculum during this Parliament.

With best wishes.

Yours sincerely,
Nick

Chapter 5

1. "Everyone must play by the same rules": CNBC, https://www.cnbc.com/2021/02/19/biden-says-us-and-europe-must-push-back-against-chinas-economic-abuses.html

2. "surpass ourselves for a better China": Chinese Ministry of Foreign Affairs Website, https://www.fmprc.gov.cn/mfa_eng/xwfw_665399/s2510_665401/t1875564.shtml

3. "China's goal has never been to surpass the U.S.": Xinhuanet, http://www.xinhuanet.com/english/2021-03/26/c_139838556.htm

4. "Yes. It requires peace among the great powers": Irish Times, https://www.irishtimes.com/business/economy/martin-wolf-why-the-tide-of-globalisation-is-turning-1.2782840

Postscript

After I finished writing the book, on the 9th of September 2021, the White House published A Readout of President Joseph R. Biden Jr's Call with President Xi Jinping of the People's Republic of China, in which it said: "President Joseph R. Biden, Jr. spoke today with President Xi Jinping of the People's Republic of China (PRC). The two leaders had a broad, strategic discussion in which they discussed areas where our interests converge, and areas where our interests, values, and perspectives diverge.

They agreed to engage on both sets of issues openly and straightforwardly. This discussion, as President Biden made clear, was part of the United States' ongoing effort to responsibly manage the competition between the United States and the PRC. President Biden underscored the United States' enduring interest in peace, stability, and prosperity in the Indo-Pacific and the world and the two leaders discussed the responsibility of both nations to ensure competition does not "veer into conflict."

It's the second time the two leaders talked after Biden went into the White House. It showed that Biden has started to try to sort out the relations with China by himself after his senior officers all failed. For the whole human history, the competition between the strongest powers have aimed for hegemony, via negotiations, attacks, wars and nuclear deterrence, in a hostile and suspicious way. The two leaders discussed the responsibility of both nations to ensure competition does not "veer into conflict" has shown a new civilized approach to International Relations. Although how much they can trust each other, is another issue.

"Readout of President Joseph R. Biden Jr. Call with President Xi Jinping of the People's Republic of China, in which said: ''President Joseph R. Biden, Jr. spoke today with President Xi Jinping of the People's Republic of China (PRC)'': White House website, https://www.whitehouse.gov/briefing-room/statements-releases/2021/09/09/readout-of-president-joseph-r-biden-jr-call-with-president-xi-jinping-of-the-peoples-republic-of-china/

Why not sign up to our mailing list here:

Find out more about Yue He Parkinson:

Why not browse our BOOKSHOP?

Find out more about Bite-Sized Books here:

Printed in Great Britain
by Amazon